SO-ACS-543

STEAM GUIDES IN INVENTIONS

Kevin Walker

Scan for Related Titles and Teacher Resources

Rourke
Educational Media
rourkeeducationalmedia.com

Before Reading:

Building Academic Vocabulary and Background Knowledge

Before reading a book, it is important to tap into what your child or students already know about the topic. This will help them develop their vocabulary, increase their reading comprehension, and make connections across the curriculum.

1. *Look at the cover of the book. What will this book be about?*
2. *What do you already know about the topic?*
3. *Let's study the Table of Contents. What will you learn about in the book's chapters?*
4. *What would you like to learn about this topic? Do you think you might learn about it from this book? Why or why not?*
5. *Use a reading journal to write about your knowledge of this topic. Record what you already know about the topic and what you hope to learn about the topic.*
6. *Read the book.*
7. *In your reading journal, record what you learned about the topic and your response to the book.*
8. *After reading the book complete the activities below.*

Content Area Vocabulary
Read the list. What do these words mean?

applications
combustion
composition
compress
data
determination
dramatic
innovation
organization
reasonable
transportation
version

After Reading:

Comprehension and Extension Activity

After reading the book, work on the following questions with your child or students in order to check their level of reading comprehension and content mastery.

1. *Is a college degree needed to become an inventor?* (Summarize)
2. *Once an invention is created and a model is built, what is the next step?* (Inferring)
3. *What is the role of a project designer?* (Asking Questions)
4. *What does STEAM stand for?* (Text to self connection)
5. *Who invented the original air conditioner?* (Asking questions)

Extension Activity

Think about all the inventions you read about in the book. Which one did you find most interesting? Take that invention and think of ways you could improve on it. Go through all the steps described in the book on how to do this. Don't forget to record each step in the process so you can successfully build a model of your new, improved invention. Did it work? Now, maybe you can think of a brand new invention!

TABLE OF CONTENTS

INTRODUCTION

Every day, each of us uses something that once existed only in the imagination of an inventor.

You can flip a switch and a light comes on, thanks to Thomas Edison. You can ride to soccer practice in a car thanks to a number of engineers, especially Karl Benz. You can cover great distances quickly in an airplane thanks to Orville and Wilbur Wright never giving up on their dream of flying. And you can walk down the street while talking on a cell phone thanks to little-known inventor Marty Cooper.

Thomas Edison
1847 – 1931

Orville Wright
1871 – 1948

Have you ever wondered who was behind famous inventions such as the car and airplane? Are you curious about how inventions are created and then sold to people like you and your friends? Are you interested in becoming an inventor?

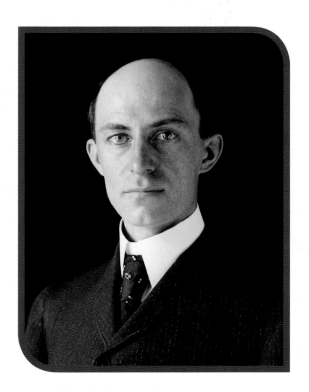

Wilbur Wright
1867 – 1912

Karl Benz
1844 – 1929

INVENTION DEPENDS ON STEAM

All inventions, from rockets that launch into space to a new kind of cell phone case, involve STEAM. That's shorthand for science, technology, engineering, art, and math.

r example, engineering
scientific understanding
odynamics—the study
w objects move through
r—allowed Orville and
ur Wright to get the first
to fly.

A better toothpaste requires the work of chemists, who study the **composition** of matter. Creating new clothing designs requires a blend of art and technology skills.

STEAM Fast Fact !

The first successful flight of Orville and Wilbur Wright's plane, the *Wright Flyer*, happened Dec. 17, 1903, near Kitty Hawk, North Carolina. Others had built planes, but the brothers were the first to make a controlled, powered, heavier-than-air flight.

Smartphones are another good example of using STEAM knowledge to invent something new. The most popular smartphone, the Apple iPhone, went on sale in 2007. Now, more than one billion smartphones are used around the world.

An Apple iPhone allows you to call, text, email, and use the Internet all from one small device.

STEAM Fast Fact!

Marty Cooper, an engineer for Motorola, created the mobile phone in 1972. He made the first public call from a mobile phone from a New York City sidewalk on April 2, 1973—to a rival engineer at AT&T Bell Laboratories!

Software developers are especially important with smartphones, creating features such as digital cameras, text messaging, and **applications**.

Perhaps the most famous use of STEAM for inventions is the manned space program in the United States.

Walking on the moon was an amazing accomplishment. Getting there required the work of experts who planned the flight and built both the spaceship and the rocket to launch it. Talk about teamwork!

In addition to the space program, inventors at the National Aeronautics and Space Administration (NASA) have also given the world other great products. They include:

• firefighter suits that are light and durable

• memory foam used in mattresses

• cordless power tools

• sneakers with more cushion

• freeze-dried food

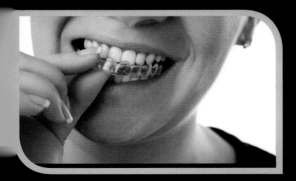
• invisible braces

• baby food preservatives

WHAT DRIVES INVENTION?

Almost all inventions are created to improve life. Three of the big areas are healthcare, **transportation**, and daily activities.

Some inventions have a **dramatic** effect on health for people worldwide. Scientist Alexander Fleming discovered that a mold could prevent growth of bacteria, which led to the infection-fighting drug penicillin. Inventive scientists continue to create medical drugs to improve health.

Alexander Fleming
1881 – 1955

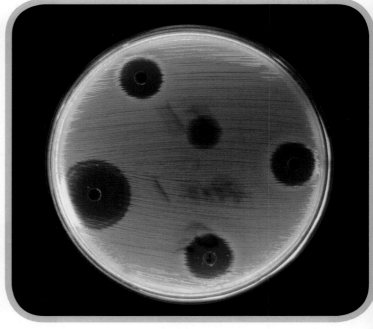

Fleming first discovered the medical potential of mold when he returned from a vacation to find fungus had grown on an experiment in his lab, killing nearby bacteria.

Benjamin Franklin
1706 – 1790

Some healthcare inventions were driven by personal concerns. Benjamin Franklin invented the flexible catheter—a thin tube that can be inserted into the body—to help extract bladder stones from his brother.

Rene Laennac
1781 – 1826

In 1815, French physician Rene Laennac invented the stethoscope because he had a patient so large that he could not hear her heartbeat by putting his ear to her chest! Now, doctors everywhere use a stethoscope daily.

Early wheels were made of stone. The first wheels—dating back to 3,500 BCE—were used as potter's wheels.

A desire to improve transportation, making it faster and more convenient, drives many inventions. This idea goes back before recorded history, when the wheel was invented.

Centuries later, the dream to improve transportation led from the steam engine to modern means: trains, planes, and automobiles.

STEAM Fast Fact!

Some inventions are so amazing that people have trouble believing them. In 1895, German physicist Wilhelm Conrad Rontgen discovered the x-ray. The *New York Times* mocked the announcement, calling Rontgen's breakthrough an "alleged discovery of how to photograph the impossible."

Leonardo da Vinci drew flying machines as early as the 15th century, but most major inventions in transportation have happened in just the past 200 years.

Invention	Year Invented
bicycle	1790
motorcycle	1867
automobile	1885
airplane	1903
helicopter	1940
manned spacecraft	1969
space shuttle	1981

The first practical, two-wheeled bicycle was the wooden draisen, invented by German Baron Karl von Drais in 1817.

Modern kitchens feature a host of inventions, including the electric oven, microwave, and refrigerator.

Some inventions improve day-to-day life, such as better cleaning products, detergents, dental care devices, and garbage bags. Bags that smell good are a recent, and very welcome, invention!

Other home inventions include dishwashers, garbage disposals, microwave ovens that can prepare meals in minutes, and refrigerators that allow everyone to safely store food at home.

STEAM Fast Fact!

The microwave oven was invented by accident. In 1945, engineer Percy Spencer conducted experiments with magnetrons, which make microwaves, when a candy bar in his pocket melted! He then heated popcorn and eggs and learned how fast microwaves heat food.

Willis Carrier
1876 – 1950

Of all the inventions that improve daily life, none were bigger than air conditioning. Invented by engineer Willis Carrier in 1902, air conditioning made living in hotter climates easier.

Air conditioning involves machines and chemistry. Modern air conditioners use a refrigerant, a chemical that cools as it moves from a liquid to gas state, which is done by a machine that can **compress** the chemical.

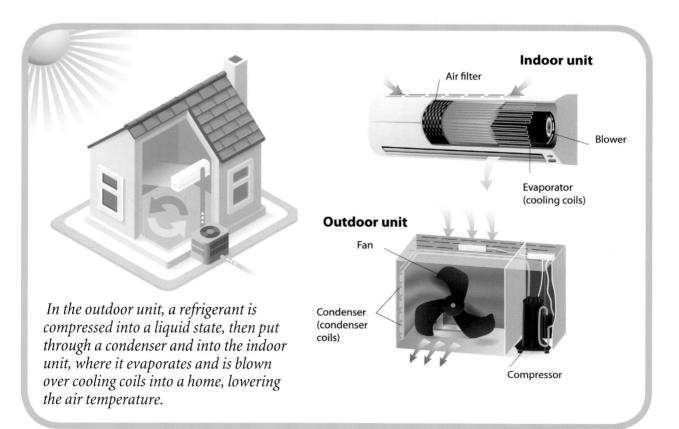

Indoor unit
Air filter
Blower
Evaporator (cooling coils)

Outdoor unit
Fan
Condenser (condenser coils)
Compressor

In the outdoor unit, a refrigerant is compressed into a liquid state, then put through a condenser and into the indoor unit, where it evaporates and is blown over cooling coils into a home, lowering the air temperature.

INVENTING THE FIRST MODEL

Most inventors start by creating the first **version** of a product themselves or working with a team. Taking an idea from their mind to reality can be a long process.

Thomas Edison, for example, famously went through more than 2,000 different versions until he made a safe, dependable light bulb. That kind of **determination** is something you see in many inventors.

Thomas Edison's laboratory is where many of his inventions were created.

Christiaan Huygens
1629 – 1695

While the names of one inventor are the best known, many new creations are the result of a team of people. Marty Cooper used ideas from his team at Motorola to create the first mobile phone. Teams of designers and engineers worked to create the Apple iPhone.

Teams of scientists work in labs to create inventions such as new medical drugs to fight disease or chronic medical conditions.

Nowhere in the process of invention does STEAM seem more important than in creating the first model.

Take the ballpoint pen. Hundreds of attempts were made to create one that worked. Inventors tried from 1888, when the first one was attempted, to 1931, when Hungarian newspaper editor Laszlo Biro and his brother, Gyorgy, a chemist, finally made one that worked well enough to sell.

STEAM Fast Fact !

Why did Laszlo Biro want a new kind of pen? Because he was tired of cleaning up the messes caused by using old-fashioned fountain pens. In some parts of Europe, a ballpoint pen is called a "biro."

Laszlo Biro
1899 – 1985

To understand how difficult it is to build a model that works, it helps to know about those who failed.

In 1647, Italian inventor Tito Livio Burattini created a flying machine that was shaped like a dragon with four pairs of wings attached. It managed to lift a cat, but not a person.

And before answering machines and voicemail, Austrian inventor Claus Scholz invented a phone-answering robot. The problem? It could not speak, only pick up and put down the phone!

WAIT! WHAT ABOUT MATH AND ART?

Scientists, engineers, and computer experts are often mentioned when discussing inventions. But what about math and art?

The truth is, without math, none of the work of inventors would be possible. All of them need an understanding of math concepts.

Charles Babbage was the first to begin working on a mechanical computing device. Alan Turing laid the groundwork for the invention of the personal computer. Both were mathematicians.

Charles Babbage
1791 – 1871

Alan Turing
1912 – 1954

Math is also behind technology. For example, almost everyone has searched for something on the Internet using Google, but did you know that Google uses complex math—called algorithms—and computer code to decide your search results?

The bottom line: Before actually creating anything new, scientists and engineers first have to use math concepts.

```
11   var b = count_array_gen();
12   parseInt(liczenie().unique);
13   var c = array_bez_powt(), a = " ", d = parseInt(
14   function("LIMIT_total:" + d);
15   function("rand:" + f);
16   d < f && (f = d, function("check rand\u00f3\u00f
17   var h = [], d = d - f, e;
18   if (0 < c.length) {
19      for (var g = 0;g < c.length;g++) {
20         e = indexOf_Array(b, c[g]), -1 < e && b.spli
21      }
22      for (g = 0;g < c.length;g++) {
23         b.unshift({use_class:"parameter", word:c[g]}
24      }
25   }
26   e = indexOf_keyword(b, " ");
27   -1 < e && b.splice(e, 1);
28   e = indexOf_keyword(b, void 0);
29   -1 < e && b.splice(e, 1);
30   e = indexOf_keyword(b, "");
31   -1 < e && b.splice(e, 1);
2    for (c = 0;c < d && c < b.length;c++) {
        a += b[c].word + " ", b.push(b[c].word)
```

(Above) Computer code is a symbolic language using text and numbers to program computers. (Below) Math provides the foundation for many scientific breakthroughs and inventions.

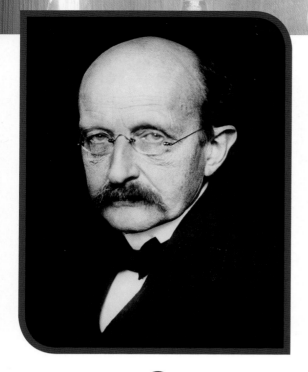

Art also is important to **innovation**. A University of Michigan study found that students educated in the arts often went on to create new inventions and form new companies.

Max Planck
1858 – 1947

Max Planck, who created quantum physics—the study of the smallest particles that make up things—said "the creative scientist needs an artistic imagination."

Today, many scientists protest against the cutting of arts funding in schools because they know the importance of art and creativity.

Art is important not only in the design of inventions, but also, in the marketing and selling of them.

So, just because you enjoy and excel in art and writing does not mean you can't also do well in science and math! The arts can help you better prepare for becoming an inventor.

Doing arts and crafts projects can tap into your creative side, and also may prepare you for leadership and invention.

Other studies have found that education in the arts leads to skills such as observing, imagination, and seeing patterns in images and objects.

Leonardo da Vinci
1452 – 1519

The Last Supper by Leonardo da Vinci

Copyright, 1878, by MUYBRIDGE.

THE HORSE IN MOTION.

MORSE'S Gallery, 417 Montgomery St., San Francisco.

Photos by Eadweard Muybridge

Eadweard Muybridge, a creative photographer, invented cameras able to capture objects in motion. Max Fleischer, an artist and cartoonist, invented Rotoscope, one of the early machines used to make animated films.

And Steve Jobs, creator of famous Apple products, thought design and art were critical to creating new products.

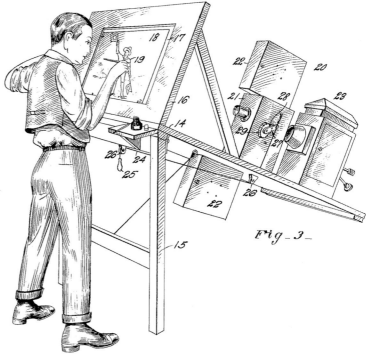

An illustration of the Rotoscope, invented by Max Fleischer (1883 – 1972).

GETTING A PATENT

Once an invention has been created and a successful first model built, it's time to get a patent, which officially records the invention. In the United States, this is done by the U.S. Patent and Trademark Office.

An important step is to keep records of the process used to create an invention. It's also important to make sure someone has not already filed a patent for the same invention.

An important part of seeking a patent is making sure that the product meets the rules for getting one.

The law for patents explains that they are for "new and useful" inventions.

Another important rule: You cannot get a patent for an invention that was made available for sale before you received a patent.

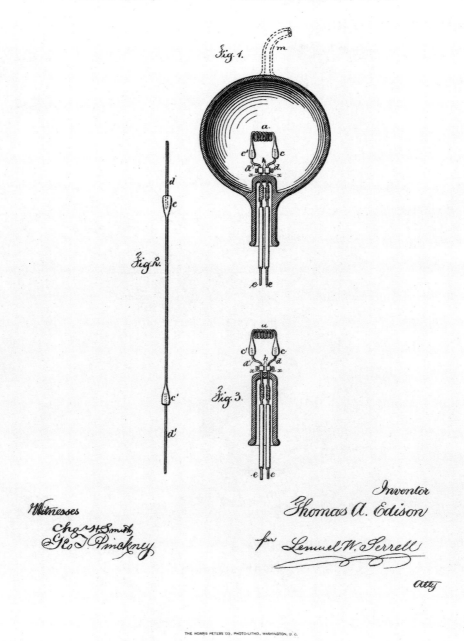

T. A. EDISON.
Electric-Lamp.

No. 223,898.   Patented Jan. 27, 1880.

Fig. 1.

Fig. 2.

Fig. 3.

Witnesses
Chas. H. Smith
Geo. T. Pinckney

Inventor
Thomas A. Edison

for Lemuel W. Serrell
Atty

THE NORRIS PETERS CO., PHOTO-LITHO., WASHINGTON, D. C.

Thomas Edison had more than 2,300 patents worldwide. More than 1,000 of these were U.S. patents.

There are more than half a million patents granted in the U.S. every year.

There have been patents filed in recent years for ways to make ocean water drinkable, cars that stop when drivers don't pay attention to the road, life-like animal robots, and an emergency medical response drone.

In some desalination plants, water flows through a set of filters to separate salt. Water is moved with high pressure through semipermeable membranes in a process called reverse osmosis, which filters out salt molecules.

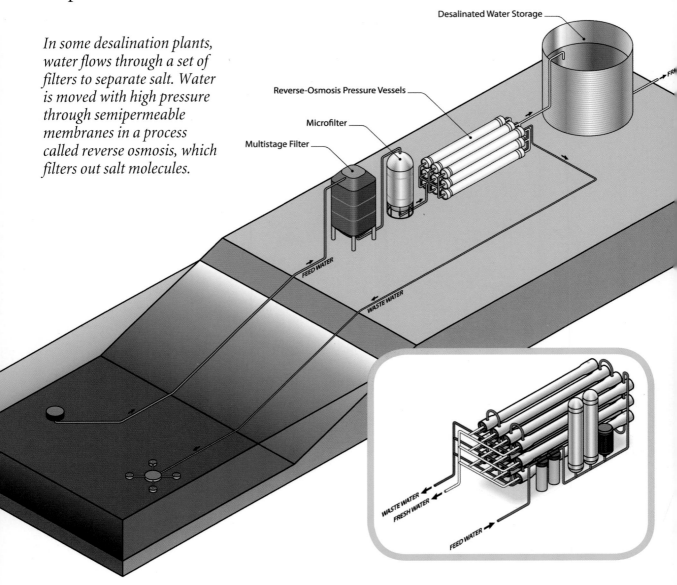

Desalinated Water Storage

Reverse-Osmosis Pressure Vessels

Microfilter

Multistage Filter

FEED WATER

WASTE WATER

WASTE WATER
FRESH WATER
FEED WATER

Though still new, emergency response drones could allow for faster response to accidents, natural disasters and mountain rescues. Drones can carry a medical toolbox and also communicate with people at the scene using an onboard camera connected to medical staff operating the drone.

TESTING THE INVENTION

Before you can buy them off the shelf, all products must go through a testing process. This means inventors must turn over their invention to engineers and scientists who put the product through tough tests.

They have two main questions to answer about the invention: "Does it work?" and "Is it safe?"

In general, there are three places where new inventions are tested, although not every product is always tested by each one.

The first is the industry itself. Almost every industry has a trade **organization**, a group that promotes the industry and may also develop safety and performance standards. This is called self-regulation.

A worker tests an electronic circuit board.

The government also plays a role. This is done through laws that create safety standards, so that every invention is safe to buy.

Testing is typically done by the manufacturer, and government agencies often oversee results.

The federal Food and Drug Administration approves all new medical drugs in the United States.

Consumer protection organizations test products to see if they are safe. One of the most popular is *Consumer Reports*, which offers reviews of everything from automobiles to electronic appliances.

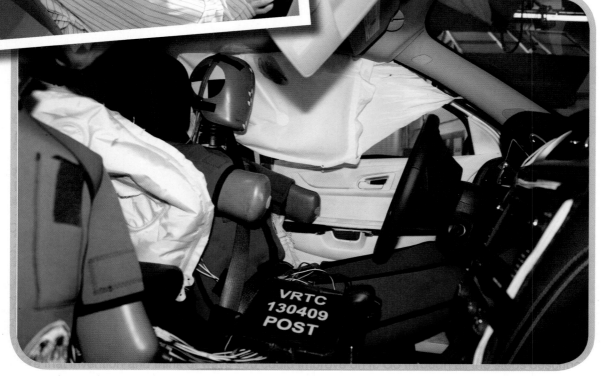

Crash test dummies equipped with electronic sensors are used to test the safety of every model of car and truck.

Scientists, particularly those who work in chemistry and biology, create new medical drugs that help people combat diseases and medical conditions.

Approval for medical drugs takes time. The inventors must first test the drug, send findings to the government, test the drugs on animals or in laboratory tests, test the drugs on a small group of people, and then get final approval.

Inventing a new medical drug can take years of lab work and tests.

DESIGNING AND MARKETING INVENTIONS

Once a product is approved to be sold to the public, that's when other people with STEAM skills get involved.

Product design is important, and this is where those with artistic skills often work. Teams of designers develop how a product looks, from the packaging to the logo.

After a product is designed and ready to sell, the marketing department steps in. It is their efforts, often called a marketing campaign, which bring the product to your attention.

Marketing also requires STEAM skills—particularly math, technology and art.

Marketing strategy involves an overall, planned message that is delivered via websites, social media, television, radio, and print publications.

STEAM Fast Fact!

Writers are important when it comes to new inventions. They come up with ideas for the name of the product as well as descriptions of how it works. Their work is used for advertising, websites, and on the product's packaging.

People in marketing study demographics to learn about the behavior of people in different age, gender, and economic groups.

Those who are good with math and statistics use their skills to analyze **data** about demographics, the study of groups within large populations. They look at things such as the age and buying habits of people who might be interested in the new product.

As more shoppers buy products on the Internet, people are needed who work well on computers. Software programs record information about people who visit a website. Some programs can also show how long visitors stayed on a website and whether they bought any of your products.

Marketing plays an important role in bringing an invention to the attention of the public. Without the efforts of those who work in marketing, great inventions would never be discovered by people who wish to own them.

People can see an advertisement and immediately purchase an item from their smartphone.

Advertising, like that in Times Square in New York City, is used to communicate a positive message about an item for sale.

SELLING AND DELIVERING NEW PRODUCTS

At this point, an invention that started in the mind of a creator has been built, tested, found to be safe, designed beautifully, and a marketing campaign has been created.

Automated machinery, a 20th century invention, moves boxes full of merchandise in factories.

While an item in a store might catch your eye, it is usually what's on the price tag that most influences your decision.

Selling an invention requires technology and math. Data is used to find the places to best sell the product.

Mathematics and statistics are used to find a **reasonable** price for an item. Companies want to make money, but they also don't want to charge so much people will not buy a product. Experts review pricing data to determine how much to charge.

In the not-too-distant future, items you order online may be delivered to your home by a drone.

How to deliver the items also has become a focus for people with education in STEAM. Many people already buy items online, and we have learned the importance of STEAM in creating websites.

Now two Internet-based companies, Amazon and Google, are looking at delivering products that are purchased online by taking them to your home with remote-controlled drones.

Television commercials and newspaper advertisements are still used to sell products, but many companies sell new products through social media or websites.

This is where those with good technology and communication skills are important, reaching people who are interested in the product through avenues such as Facebook, Twitter, and Instagram.

Smartphone apps for online stores and social media are developed by people with STEAM skills.

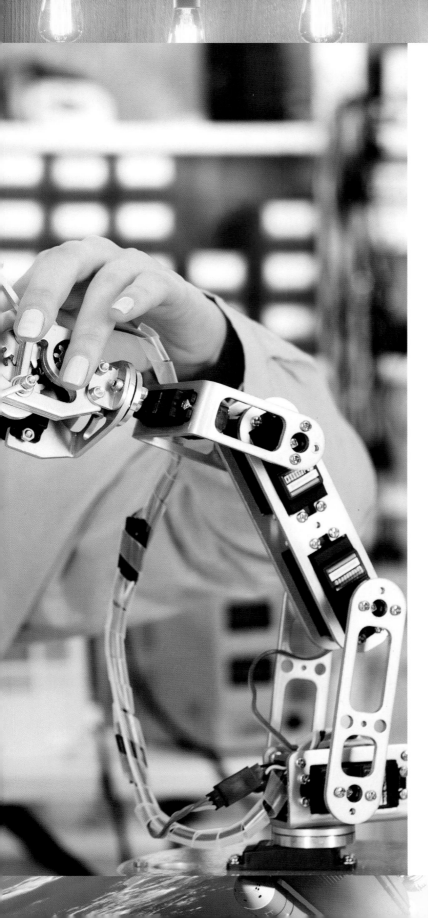

The love of invention is one of the most interesting things about people. Much like paintings or books, inventions spring from the minds of those who dream of creating something from an idea.

Now you know the steps it takes to take an invention from an idea to the market. Maybe the next great invention will come from your imagination!

GLOSSARY

applications (ap-li-KAY-shuhns): computer programs that perform a certain task

combustion (kuhm-BUS-chuhn): the process of burning

composition (kahm-puh-ZISH-uhn): the combining of parts to form a whole

compress (kuhm-PRES): to press or flatten something in order to fit it into a smaller space

data (DAY-tuh): information collected in a place so something can be done with it

determination (di-tur-muh-NAY-shuhn): a strong will to do something

dramatic (druh-MAT-ik): very noticeable

innovation (in-uh-VAY-shuhn): a new idea or invention

organization (or-guh-ni-ZAY-shuhn): a number of people joined together for a particular purpose

reasonable (REE-zuh-nuh-buhl): the process of thinking in an orderly fashion, drawing conclusions from facts

transportation (trans-pur-TAY-shuhn): a means or system of moving people or freight from one place to another

version (VUR-zhuhn): a different or changed form of something, such as a book or software

INDEX

SHOW WHAT YOU KNOW

1. Many people worked on the automobile, but who is credited with inventing the one that directly led to the modern car?
2. Chemists are important in the creation of many inventions. Can you name an invention chemists helped create?
3. Name three jobs that are related to an education in STEAM—science, technology, engineering, art, and math.
4. What are the three areas of STEAM most used in marketing?
5. Is it true or false that in order to get a patent, an invention must be useful in some way?

WEBSITES TO VISIT

http://stem-works.com
http://www.nasa.gov/audience/forstudents/index.html
http://www.egfi-k12.org

ABOUT THE AUTHOR

Kevin Walker is a father, editor, and writer living in Texas. He wishes he had invented the Hula Hoop, because it's just for fun. Or maybe cotton candy.

Meet The Author!
www.meetREMauthors.com

PHOTO CREDITS: Cover lightbulbs © 4Max, rocket © 3Dsculptor; pages 4-5 courtesy Library of Congress except Martin Cooper © Rico Shen; page 6-7 NASA/Bill Ingalls), page 7 flight at kitty Hawk courtesy Library of Congress;page 8 © Denys Prykhodov, page 8-9 texting © vectorfusionart, apps © Stefano Garau, self © Odua Images; page 10 courtesy of NASA, page 11 firefighter suit © curraheeshutter, mattress © Will Thomass, drill © kola, sneakers © SergANTstar, raspberries © neil langan, braces © Lucky Business, baby food © Gayvoronskaya_Yana; Page 12 Alexander Fleming courtesy of Imperial War Museum, antibiotics test plate © CDC / Provider: Don Stalons; page 13 © Rocketclips, Inc; page 14 © John O'Neill, page 14-15 car © Kurmyshov; page 15 bicycle © Gun Powder Ma, motorcycle © Wladyslaw, car © DaimlerChrysler AG, helicopter © NASA/NACA, LARC, Apollo 8 and Space Shuttle © NASA; page 16 cleaning products © Africa Studio, kitchen © Breadmaker, page 17 photo units © Carolyn Franks, illustrations © Designua, aurielaki; page 18 © Everett Historical, page 19 © wavebreakmedia; page 20 pen © Roberto Fiadone, Daniel Schwen, pen writing © Mau Horng; page 22 © Andrew Dunn: CC-BY-SA-2.0, page 23 math on chalkboard © ImageFlow, computer code © Mclek; page 24-25 © Monkey Business Images; page 30-31 desalinization plant images © Zern Liew, drone © © Chesky; page 32 © kermess, page 33 © Eight Photo; page 34 © Vereshchagin Dmitry, page 35 © Joey Chung; page 36-37 © Rawpixel.com, page 37 © g-stockstudio; page 38 © Andrey_Popov, Georgejmclittle, page 39 © Stuart Monk; page 40 © Marcin Balcerzak, page 41 © antoniodiaz, page 42 © Slavoljub Pantelic, page 43 © quake; page 45-45 © science photo. All photos from Shutterstock.com except pages 4, 5, 6, 7 (Wright Bros.), 10, 12, 13 (inventor's photos), 14, 15 (inset photos), 17 (Willis Carrier), 19 (top), 20, 22, 24, 26-29

Edited by: Keli Sipperley

Cover and Interior design by: Nicola Stratford   www.nicolastratford.com

Library of Congress PCN Data

STEAM Guides in Inventions / Kevin Walker
(STEAM Every Day)
  ISBN 978-1-68191-706-1 (hard cover)
  ISBN 978-1-68191-807-5 (soft cover)
  ISBN 978-1-68191-903-4 (e-Book)

Library of Congress Control Number: 2016932584

Rourke Educational Media
Printed in the United States of America, North Mankato, Minnesota

Also Available as:
ROURKE'S
e-Books

MAR - - 2017